TRUTH AND MASKS

ANNAMARIA COURTENAY

Text © Annamaria Courtenay 2022

Front and back cover © Cyrus Murati 2022
All images are in the public domain.
The masks on the front are from KindPNG.
The Cross on the back is from Pinclipart.

Published by Amazon's Kindle Direct Publishing in 2022.
Available in paperback and Kindle Edition.

CONTENTS

INTRODUCTION 1

ACKOWLEDGEMTS 3

TRUTH AND MASKS 5

THE DIVINE LITURGY AND COMMUNION 11

THE HOLY FATHERS ON COMMUNION 15

A PRAYER OF REPENTANCE 19

INTRODUCTION

I completed this work in the course of 2021. I wrote each item at different times and for different purposes, as evident in the variety of styles. However, the underlying theme is the same, namely, what it means to be true. I therefore decided to put the parts together into the present whole. Long absence from the Divine Liturgy and the Precious Body and Blood of God as a result of lockdowns has made it easy to forget how central these are to growing into who we truly are.

This work is accessible to older children as well as adults, provided that they have a basic knowledge of the Orthodox faith. May it benefit the souls of all who read it. I ask your prayers for my own.

If anyone should deliberately misquote or misuse my words in any way, let him remember: he cannot run away from the mirror forever.

Annamaria Courtenay
November 2021

ACKNOWLEDGEMENTS

I am grateful to Cyrus Murati for his help with publishing. The cover designs are his.

I am also grateful to those whom I consulted for giving me feedback and encouragement.

TRUTH AND MASKS

Knowledge is of two kinds: one for the head, the other for the heart. *2 + 2 = 4. Britain is an island. Everyone dies.* These are for the head. *3 = 1 (the Holy Trinity). God's Kingdom is in you. Christ is life.* These are for the heart. The difference is that the heart knows something only by *living* it, that is, when it is part of you. Words on their own cannot explain it.

A person can be true or false. Being true does not mean telling the truth neither does being false mean lying. A true person *lives* the truth. He lives as the unique person God calls him to be, his true self. A false person *lives* a lie. He lives contrary to God's calling, hiding from himself behind a mask. There is only one truth but endless masks. For example, wealth, title, family, strength, and knowledge become masks when you make them ends in themselves.

Adam and Eve believed more in Satan's lies, with their heads, than in God's commandment, with their hearts. Adam hid from his true self behind the mask of Eve (Genesis 3:12). In turn, Eve hid behind the mask of Satan (Genesis 3:13). Being made in God's image, they thereby hid God from themselves. Thus killing Life in their hearts, they gave birth to death.

God called a certain Mary to give birth to him so that he could kill death and restore his broken image in man. This Mary, the Most Holy Theotokos, was true to her calling. Her head did not understand it (Luke 1:34). However, she followed her heart (Luke 1:38). She wore no masks. Giving birth to Life, she reversed the Fall.

In this earthly life you choose whether to live the truth or a lie. Repentance means throwing off the masks and growing into your true self. Each is called to repent in a unique way. Callings mostly fall into general categories, such as priesthood, motherhood, monasticism, marriage, foolishness, martyrdom, or art. They always involve giving of yourself. You are made in the image of God, a communion of Three Persons. Hence, you find yourself only by reaching out to others and giving. If your soul 'self-isolates', you are dead in your own lie.

You need a mirror to see your true self, just as to see your face. God is the ultimate *mirror of repentance*. Monks and nuns look into it all the time through prayer. Being made in the image of God, another human being also is a mirror. A well-matched husband and wife are each other's mirrors. An inorganic image of God, such as a holy icon or the Gospel, works too. Finally, an art, especially music, writing, and acting, is a kind of mirror. Through it, the artist explores his soul. So can you yours through his creation.

In this life, you can avoid the mirror. In death, all masks fall off. Inescapably coming face to face with Christ, you see your naked soul. If you accept the truth, you are saved. If you fight against it, you damn yourself. This is the Partial Judgement.

You stay in the Partial Judgement until you accept the truth. There is no guarantee that you ever will. You can harden your heart beyond repentance. Those who repent in this life pass through judgement much more quickly than those who hide. Ghosts are souls stuck in the Partial Judgement. Our prayers help them through.

The Second Coming of Christ is the Last Judgement. All creation shall be renewed and fixed in its true state. The full truth shall be visible everywhere forever. Knowing yet hating it is the fire of hell. It is isolation. Knowing and loving it is the joy of the Kingdom. It is communion. Love is free, never forced. Freedom to love means freedom to hate.

The most difficult thing in life is to live and not lie, and not believe one's own lie.
Dostoevsky, *Demons*, Chapter 6

Christ called Judas Iscariot to be one of his twelve closest disciples. However, Judas chose money over Christ. When he realised that he had believed a lie, he swapped the mask of wealth for that of guilt. Not trusting in God's forgiveness, he hanged himself. His repentance was as false as his kiss to Christ. By contrast, Peter truly repented of denying Christ for the mask of safety. He wept bitterly and returned to his true calling as an apostle and martyr.

Joseph Stalin, the most notorious dictator of the USSR, studied at an Orthodox seminary. Rejecting God, he rose to power and persecuted the Church. He killed millions. As he was dying, his face showed unspeakable terror. He was probably facing for the first time all the suffering he had caused. By contrast, Joseph the Hesychast, a twentieth-century monk, smiled minutes after dying. He had already passed the Partial Judgement in his life on earth.

The Pharisee wears the most dangerous mask. Twisting himself to fit into a code of morality, he hides from the sickness of his soul behind his imagined virtue. Isolated as a result, he prays 'towards himself' and scorns his less perfect neighbour (Luke 18:11-12). Naturally, Christ's presence offends him. By contrast, the cheating tax collector, the adulteress, the thief, know that they are broken and in need of God. They easily accept Christ, glad to drop their uncomfortable masks, free now to grow straight.

> *This above all: to thine own self be true.*
> *And it must follow, as the night the day,*
> *Thou canst not then be false to any man.*
> **Shakespeare, *Hamlet,* Act I, Scene 3**

You can be true through a mask by using it as a tool rather than an end in itself. Actors show how frail and complex life truly is by putting on false identities. Fools-for-Christ lead people to repentance with their tricks and feigned madness. In his made-up parables, Christ speaks to our hearts. A tool-mask hides you only from others. Behind it, you know who you are. Through it, you show others who they are. The lie becomes the means to truth.

To sneak past the barrier of our hiding-masks, the mirror of repentance needs a tool-mask. On earth, Christ masked his true divine and human natures, both immortal, with human mortality. Thus, those he walked among did not suspect him to be the mirror that would rip off their beloved masks. A corner of his mask lifted at each miracle, teaching, call, prayer, warning. In response, people either dropped or clung harder to theirs.

TRUTH AND MASKS

The more you discern truth from masks, the more God shows himself. When Christ took off his mortal mask on Mount Tabor, the three disciples fell down (Matthew 17:6). Saul of Tarsus was blinded for three days after the Risen Christ appeared to him (Acts 9:1-9). To see God's full glory before you are ready would kill you. He shows only enough to kill your masks.

God tricked the ultimate mask, namely Death, Hades, the place where God is not. Hiding in his mortal body, he was able to enter Death. Having left his mask on earth, he revealed himself as God, exploding Death from within. He rose up in his true human body, changed from its mortal state, with all who accepted him. He offers his Risen Body and Blood to transform you bit by bit into your true self, made in his image. When Truth himself becomes literally part of you, the Fall is reversed and the Kingdom fulfilled within you.

THE DIVINE LITURGY AND COMMUNION

Most assuredly, I say to you, unless you eat the flesh of the Son of Man and drink his blood, you have no life in you. Whoever feeds on[1] my flesh and drinks my blood has eternal life, and I will raise him up at the last day.
John 6:53-54

      The Divine Liturgy is the Kingdom of God. God's whole plan for our salvation is played out in symbolic actions through which he manifests himself. The purpose is not to relax, not to instruct, not to produce 'moral citizens'. It is to manifest God and his Kingdom. Each part increasingly manifests, culminating in Communion. The Divine Liturgy is where God offers *himself* to us in order to raise us from our

---

[1] Most translations write 'eats.' However, here and henceforth in the Gospel chapter, Christ switches to a stronger term, which comes from *trogein*, literally, 'to chew on', 'to munch.' It indicates repetitive action. The change of word is very deliberate. We are to commune not just once but frequently.

fallen state to his height, from death to life. It is the meeting point of heaven and earth, God and man. It reunites all creation with God. Irreconcilable with a self-seeking, secular world, it is not about us but about God.

The Kingdom of God is a mystery. We solve a problem by analysing it from the outside. We understand a mystery from the inside, through experience. Hence, the Kingdom is manifest only to those who experience it. We do so by being fully united with God, body *and* soul. We must give ourselves to God as entirely as he gives himself to us. We must choose to enter God and we must let God enter us. Thus, the whole point and fulfilment of the Divine Liturgy is Communion: receiving God into our souls and bodies. For that moment we are wholly united with him and one another in his Kingdom. It is a foretaste of the Resurrection.

The Greek for 'liturgy', *leitourgia*, means 'work (*ergon*) of the people (*leitos*)'. Everyone plays a role. There are no spectators, only *participants* in the drama of reality. Collaborating is essential. The priest cannot offer the sacrifice without the 'amen' of the people. The people cannot receive Christ without the priest's voice and hands. The other clergy and the servers also play their part. He who merely watches is like a man observing a family feast through a window. He remains hungry and alone. The catechumens, who worship without communing, are like servants. They share in the familial joy but not as equals, lacking the experience of the meal itself. Those who commune but resist worshipping are thieves. Unrightfully acquiring the food, they remain outcasts by their own will. We receive in the degree to which we participate.

Love makes us grow. By frequent Communion, we grow into God. Just as God the Son became man without losing his Godhead or Personhood, we each become God without losing our humanity or uniqueness. Becoming God is called *theosis*. Neither do we replace God nor does he replace us. Made in God's image, we become more fully ourselves. Like branches grafted onto a tree, inseparable yet distinct from it, we could not blossom into who we are without the life derived from God. Our potential for growth is as limitless as God. Salvation is forever dynamic. It is *theosis*. Damnation is eternal stagnation. It is remaining a mere man.

No one is worthy of God's Kingdom. Salvation is not a matter of worthiness but of desire. God offers himself to us because he desires us. However, he never forces himself upon us. This would be rape, not love. He leaves each of us free to decide: *Do I want God? Shall I grasp his outstretched hand?* As in all true love, no virtue can commend us in his eyes and no fault or weakness can disqualify us. Our desire for him is *all* that counts. He who communes without wanting God or believing in his Body and Blood communes to his damnation. This is the kiss of Judas. Communion is not irresistible 'magic'. God enters and changes us only insofar as we let him. We can resist his love. Our salvation is in our hands.

THE HOLY FATHERS ON COMMUNION

Athanasius the Great (c. 296 - 373)
The Son of God became man, that we might become God.

[Theosis is] becoming by grace what God is by nature.
- On the Incarnation, I

Irenaeus, Bishop of Lyons (b. 130)
For man is made in the image of God, and the image of God is the Son, according to whose image man was made; and for this reason, he appeared in the last times, to render the image like himself.
- On the Apostolic Preaching, I

Cyril, Patriarch of Jerusalem (313 - 386)
For this Bread goeth not into the belly and is cast out into the draught [Matthew 15:17], but is diffused through all that you are, for the benefit of soul and body.
- Mystagogical Catecheses, 5:15

Maximos the Confessor (c. 580 - 662)

God has created us in order that we may become partakers of the divine nature, in order that we may enter into eternity, and that we may appear like unto him, being deified by that grace out of which all things that exist have come, and which brings into existence everything that before had no existence.

- Epistle 43

[H]e who prays to receive this supersubstantial Bread does not receive it altogether as this Bread is in itself, but as he is able to receive it. For the Bread of Life, out of his love for men, gives himself to all who ask him, but not in the same manner to everyone. To those who have done great works, he gives himself more fully; to those who have done smaller ones, less. To each, then, according to the spiritual dignity enabling him to receive it.

- Commentary on the Our Father

[F]or those who are born from above through the Spirit from an incorruptible seed, [the Bread of Life] becomes true spiritual milk. For those who are infirm, it is a herb which soothes the passive faculty of the soul. For those who, through habit, have trained the soul's spiritual sense to discern good and evil, he gives himself as solid nourishment. The Word of God has also other infinite powers [...]. For the highest of any of the

spiritual gifts given by God in this life is modest and trifling in comparison with those to come.
- *Chapters on Knowledge,* 1:100

Ephraim the Syrian (c. 306 - c. 373)
Yet I intend to approach the all-pure and terrifying Mysteries of thy Son and God, and therefore do I suffer fear, and trembling embraces me because of the unbearable multitude of my sins. But if ever I am to remain without Communion on the pretext of my unworthiness, then shall I fall into a great abyss of evil and bring upon myself great chastisement.
- *A Spiritual Psalter,*
Prayer 111 (to the Theotokos)

A PRAYER OF REPENTANCE

Lord Jesus Christ, I am fallen: raise me up.
Lord Jesus Christ, I am broken: restore me.
Lord Jesus Christ, I am weak: strengthen me.

O Lord, have mercy on me; heal my soul, for I have sinned against thee.[1]

Lord Jesus Christ, I am deaf: unblock mine ears.
Lord Jesus Christ, I am blind: open mine eyes.
Lord Jesus Christ, I am dumb: unloose my tongue.

O Lord, have mercy on me; heal my soul, for I have sinned against thee.

Lord Jesus Christ, I am fettered: free me.
Lord Jesus Christ, I am naked: clothe me.
Lord Jesus Christ, I am hungry: feed me.

O Lord, have mercy on me; heal my soul, for I have sinned against thee.

---

[1] During Pascha, say instead: *Christ is risen from the dead, trampling down death by death, and upon those in the tombs bestowing life.*

Lord Jesus Christ, I need thee: come to me.
Lord Jesus Christ, I love thee: abide in me.
Lord Jesus Christ, I want thee: manifest thyself.[1]

O Lord, have mercy on me; heal my soul, for I have sinned against thee.

---

[1] Not an external manifestation but internal, that is, the death and life of Christ become your own. See, for example, John 12:20-26 and 14:22-24. The Greeks and Judas are thinking in external, abstract terms. In reply, Christ speaks about seeing with the heart, by participating. What good is it to see him with your eyes if your heart remains blind?

ABOUT THE AUTHOR
Annamaria Courtenay currently attends an Orthodox parish in London, England. All profits from sales of this book will go to support this parish.

Printed in Great Britain
by Amazon